DISCOVER THROUGH CRAFT

PLANTS

By Jen Green

FRANKLIN WATTS
LONDON · SYDNEY

First published in 2014 by Franklin Watts
Franklin Watts
338 Euston Road
London NW1 3BH

Franklin Watts Australia
Level 17/207 Kent Street
Sydney, NSW 2000

Series editor: Amy Stephenson
Series designer: Jeni Child
Crafts: Rita Storey
Craft photography: Tudor Photography
Picture researcher: Diana Morris

Picture credits:
Amenic181/Shutterstock: 1. Blue Ring Media/Shutterstock: 18c.
Franck Boston/Shutterstock: 19b. Mark Bridger/Shutterstock: 19t.
Carlos Caetano/Shutterstock: 10c. Chaiwathphotos/Shutterstock:
30b. Nati Cheronova/Shutterstock: 28b. Danicek/Shutterstock:
20bl. Tomas Delano/Shutterstock: 23t. Design Natures istockphoto:
11t. Doczky/Shutterstock: 18-19 bg. Evarin 20/Shutterstock: 14bl.
Anton Foltin/Shutterstock: 5cl. Fotokostic/Shutterstock: 8. Marina
Gran/Shutterstock: 10-11bg. Richard Griffin/Shutterstock: 24t. J
Helgason/Shutterstock: 28b. Jerry Horbert/Shutterstock: 27t. Lil
Kar/Shutterstock: front cover c. Art Konovalov/Shutterstock: 27b.
Jakub Krechowicz/Shutterstock: 26-27bg. K Kulikov/Shutterstock:
22. Leptospira/Shutterstock: 16t. Dr Alan Lipkin/Shutterstock: 31t.
Gabrielle Maltini/Shutterstock: 18b. Marques/Shutterstock: 11b.
Dawna Moore/Dreamstime: 5b. Nejron Photo/Shutterstock: 12t.
Hein Nouwens/Shutterstock: front cover tr. Ollirg/Shutterstock: 12b.
Marci Paravia/Shutterstock: 32b. PHB.cz (Richard Semik)/Shutterstock:
7b, 15cr. photka/Shutterstock: 28c. Photohouse/Shutterstock:
12-13 bg. Denis and Yulia Pogostins/Shutterstock: 7t. puchan/
Shutterstock: 4. Samarttiw/Shutterstock: 5c. Gary Saxe/Shutterstock:
14br. skyfotostock/Shutterstock: 22-23bg Smitt/istockphoto: 16c.
Kuttelvaserova Stuchelova/Shutterstock: 15tl. D J Taylor/Shutterstock:
24b. Simon Thomas/Dreasmtime: 20cl. Hoang Tran/Shutterstock:
26t. Triff/Shutterstock: 6-7bg. Vasily Vashnevskiy/Shutterstock: 23b.
Vaclac Voirab/Shutterstock: 20tl. Vovan/Shutterstock: 6. Zimowa/
Shutterstock: 5cr.

Dewey number: 580
HB ISBN: 978 1 4451 3103 0
Library eBook ISBN: 978 1 4451 3584 7

Printed in China

Franklin Watts is a division of Hachette
Children's Books, an Hachette UK company.
www.hachette.co.uk

CONTENTS

Words in **bold** can be found in the glossary on page 30.

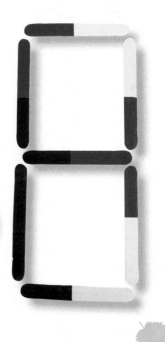

Some of the projects in this book require scissors, paint and glue. We would recommend that children are supervised by a responsible adult when using these things.

A WORLD OF PLANTS

Plants are one of the main types of living thing on Earth. Plants make the world green and leafy. They help to keep the air healthy, and also supply us with food.

Trees, grasses, bushes and wild flowers, such as these red poppies and blue cornflowers, are all different types of plant.

Variety

Scientists have identified over 300,000 different types of plant. The biggest group are the flowering plants. As well as garden flowers, this group includes grasses, **shrubs** and trees such as oak trees. Other plant groups are ferns, mosses and trees called **conifers**, which have cones.

HAVE A GO

Take a walk in a park or garden. List all the different plants you see. Remember that shrubs, grasses, trees and **crops**, such as vegetables, are all plants.

Where do plants grow?

Plants grow all over the world in many different places. These places are called **habitats**. Plants thrive in forests, woodlands and on plains. They also grow in harsh places, such as in dry deserts and on high mountains.

Aquatic plants, such as duckweed, grow in water. Some plants can even survive in very cold or snowy places. The plants that grow in each habitat are suited to the conditions there.

Cactus plants grow in deserts.

Lotus flowers grow in ponds.

An **alpine** flower on a mountain.

Big and small

Plants come in many shapes, sizes and colours. The smallest plants are duckweeds. Some only grow a few millimetres long. The biggest plants are mighty trees. Some can grow over 50 metres tall.

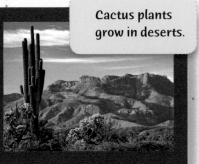

Tiny duckweed plants float on the surface of a pond.

QUIZ TIME!

Which of these is a plant?

   a. frog
   b. mushroom
   c. carrot

Answer on page 32.

Quick FACTS

• There are over 300,000 different types of plant.
• The main group are the flowering plants.
• Plants are suited to the habitat in which they live.

WHAT DO PLANTS NEED?

All plants need certain things to grow strong and healthy.

Light

All living things need sunlight to survive. Plants use energy from sunlight to make their own food – a process called **photosynthesis** (p. 12). Plants that don't get enough light become weak, pale and spindly. All plants grow upwards, towards the light.

HAVE A GO
Cover a patch of grass with a doormat or an old square of carpet to stop light from reaching the grass. Remove the cover after a week. What has happened to the patch of grass without sunlight? What happens next if you leave the same patch of grass uncovered?

Trees in a forest grow tall to reach the light.

Water

All plants need water, which they take in through their roots. The water falls as rain or is stored underground. In some hot and dry places, which have little rain and water, farmers **irrigate** their crops. Water for irrigation is taken from streams, rivers or wells. Desert plants, such as cactuses, can survive with very little water, but no plant can live without any water at all.

Gardeners water plants in dry weather to keep them alive.

Warmth

Heat from the Sun allows plants to sprout and grow. Plants grow fastest in warm weather, so summer is the main time for growing in many parts of the world. Gardeners put young plants in a greenhouse to keep them warm and help them survive through the winter.

Plants thrive in the warm conditions inside a greenhouse.

Air

Plants need a gas called **carbon dioxide** from the air to make food and grow. As they make food they give off **oxygen**, which all animals (including humans) need to breathe. So plants keep the air healthy as they live and grow.

? What else do you think plants need?
? Turn the page to find out.

Nutrients

Soil supplies the **nutrients** plants need to grow. These nutrients are called **minerals** and plants only need tiny amounts of them. On farms where crops are grown in the same fields year after year, nutrients in the soil get used up. Sometimes farmers add **fertilisers** that have nutrients in them to the soil, to help more crops grow.

A farmer adds fertiliser to the soil to give the growing plants more nutrients.

Quick FACTS

• Plants need five things to grow strong and healthy: sunlight, warmth, water, air and nutrients.
• Plants get nutrients from the soil.

QUIZ TIME!

When a plant hasn't had enough sunlight or water it starts:

    a. writing

    b. wilting

    c. quilting

Answer on page 32.

Make this

When you buy plants, they usually come with a label to show you what they need, including how much water and sunlight they like. Why not make your own plant-care labels for your plants?

Place the handle of the spoon into the soil in your plant pot. What other fun plant label ideas can you make?

1 Cut out a flower or leaf shape and two wings from coloured paper as shown.

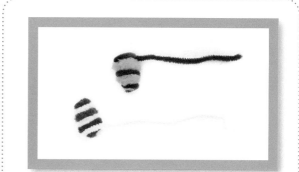

2 To make each bee, wrap one half of a brightly-coloured pipe cleaner around a small, coloured pom-pom.

3 Paint an old wooden spoon or lolly stick with poster paint and leave it to dry. Stick on your flower or leaf. Wrap the end of a bee's pipe cleaner around the spoon's handle or the lolly stick.

4 Stick two googly eyes and two wings onto each bee as shown. With a felt-tip pen, write on the instructions for care of the plant – for example: shady spot; water every other day.

SHADY SPOT; WATER EVERY OTHER DAY

PARTS OF A PLANT

An oak tree and a daisy look very different, but they have the same parts. Each of these parts has a very important job to do.

Some of this tree's huge roots are visible above the ground, but most of its roots are deep underground.

Roots

Plant roots spread down through the soil. They anchor the plant firmly in the ground, so it does not fall over in strong winds or wash away after heavy rain. The bigger the plant, the thicker and stronger the roots need to be. Trees have thick, woody roots and small plants have delicate, thread-like roots. The roots also suck up water, which also contains nutrients.

Stem

A plant's stem carries the leaves and flowers. It turns the leaves to face the Sun so they can **absorb** sunlight (p. 12). Water sucked up by the roots travels up the stem to reach other parts of the plant. Small plants, such as daisies, have a green stem. Shrubs have a woody stem. A tree's stem is its trunk, which is covered with bark. Bark protects the softer wood inside.

Thorns or prickles on the stem of some plants protect them from being eaten by animals.

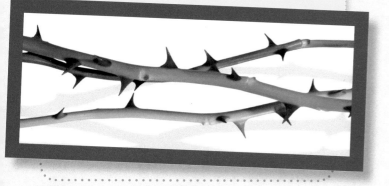

Flowers

Flowers brighten our woodlands, parks and gardens. Their colourful petals and sweet smells attract bees, butterflies and other insects. But they are not just pretty decoration. Flowers play a vital part in a plant's **life cycle**. They are needed to make fruits and seeds (pp. 18–19).

Roses attract insects with their bright petals and sweet smell.

HAVE A GO

Investigate how water travels up plant stems by adding a drop of red food colouring to a jar of water. Put white flowers, such as carnations or daisies, in the jar. The coloured water slowly travels up the stem to turn the flowers pink.

? How are a plant's leaves useful? Turn the page to find out.

Leaves

Green leaves make the plant's food, which it needs to live and grow. Tiny **veins** inside each leaf help to move this food around. Leaves are like miniature factories that run on **solar energy**. They absorb energy from sunlight, and use it to turn water, nutrients and carbon dioxide from the air into sugary food. This amazing process is called photosynthesis.

The veins in a leaf carry food and water. Look closely at a leaf to see the veins.

Leaves use energy from sunlight to make the plant's food.

Quick FACTS

• Plants have four main parts: roots, stem, leaves and flowers.
• Leaves make the plant's food.

QUIZ TIME!

Petals are a part of the flower head, but they are actually brightly coloured:

a. seeds
b. roots
c. leaves

Answer on page 32.

Make this

The fruits, stems, seeds and flowers of some plants can be eaten safely. Use these plant parts to make a healthy picture that you can eat!

You could make another plant picture using some different edible plants.

1 Use celery (stems), lettuce and watercress or other salad leaves to make trees and bushes on a plate.

2 Use carrot sticks and circles (root) and pieces of tomato and pepper (fruits) to make the Sun and a butterfly.

3 Sprinkle some pumpkin seeds at the bottom to make the soil.

! Make sure you only use edible plants - check they are OK to eat before you eat them!

4 Add edible flower petals to the Sun to make your salad really bright and fun! Now eat your healthy picture.

TREES

Trees are the biggest living things on Earth. There are three main types of tree: conifers, broad-leaved trees and palm trees.

Conifers

Pine, spruce and redwood are all types of conifers. These trees have narrow, waxy leaves, sometimes called needles. The leaves stay on the tree all year round. For this reason these trees are sometimes called **evergreens**. Conifers make their seeds inside cones rather than inside flowers.

Pine cones are hard and woody. They contain winged seeds.

Tall redwood conifers in a forest in California, USA.

Broad-leaved trees

Broad-leaved trees are named after their wide, flat leaves. There can be thousands of leaves on each fully-grown tree. Oak, beech and maple are types of broad-leaved tree. They are **deciduous**, which means they lose their leaves each autumn. They look different in each season (p. 16).

A beech tree's leaves turn orange in the autumn before they fall off the tree.

Palm trees

There are over 2,500 different types of palm tree. These trees mostly grow in warm countries. Their trunks are thin and very straight. Palm trees don't have any branches. A tall fan of leaves sprouts from the top of the trunk.

Some types of palm tree, such as these coconut palms, grow on beaches in hot countries.

Tree records

The world's tallest trees are conifers called redwoods (left) which grow in western North America. The tallest of them all is a coast redwood in California that is 115 metres tall! The shortest trees are dwarf willows, which grow in the icy **Arctic**. They are only a few centimetres tall. The world's oldest trees are bristlecone pines. These North American trees may be 5,000 years old.

Quick FACTS

• The three main types of tree are broad-leaved trees, conifers and palm trees.
• All trees are either evergreen or deciduous.

? How do broad-leaved trees change through the year? Turn the page to find out.

The leaves on a maple tree are different colours in different seasons.

Seasonal changes

Broad-leaved trees change with the seasons. In spring, leaves begin to grow. In summer, trees are green and leafy. In autumn, the tree sheds its leaves to save energy and water. Its leaves turn red and yellow and then fall off the tree. In winter, these trees are bare. More new leaves grow again in the spring.

Spring

Summer

Autumn

Winter

HAVE A GO

Work out a tree's height with a ruler! Ask a friend to stand next to a tree. Walk 30 paces away, then hold the ruler upright at arm's length. Mark your friend's height and the tree's height on the ruler. Divide the larger number on the ruler by the smaller number. Write this figure down. To find the height of the tree, multiply this figure by your friend's real height.

QUIZ TIME!

The tallest redwood in the world is so special it has been given a name. What is it called?

a. **Hyperion**
b. **General Sherman**
c. **Peter**

Answer on page 32.

Make this

Pine cones are brilliant for all kinds of crafty projects. Make a pair of cute hedgehogs for a seasonal display.

1 Roll a piece of clay or brown plasticine into a ball.

2 Pull some of the clay into a point to make the hedgehog's nose.

3 Push the flat end of a pine cone into the round end of the ball of clay. Squash the edges into the cone to keep it in place.

4 Roll a small piece of clay into a sausage shape. Bend it into a curved shape. Flatten each end and make marks for the toes.

5 Attach the feet under the cone, just behind the nose. Push black beads into the clay for the eyes and nose. Repeat steps 1–5 to make another hedgehog.

What other animals can you make from parts of a tree? You could try using twigs, leaves or bark. Could you make a bird using leaves for feathers?

FLOWERS, FRUITS AND SEEDS

Flowering plants reproduce by making flowers, fruits and seeds. But they can't reproduce without making pollen first.

Parts of a flower

Flowers contain the parts needed for **reproduction**. Inside the petals, male parts called **stamens** produce **pollen**. In the centre is a stalk called the **stigma**. At the base of the flower is a hollow case called the **ovary**. This female part contains eggs, which will develop into seeds if they are **fertilised** with the male pollen.

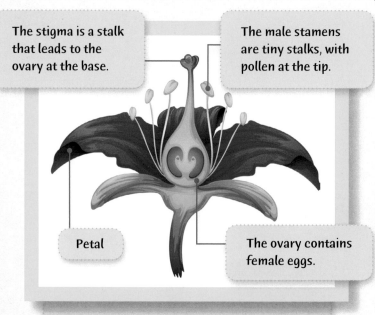

The stigma is a stalk that leads to the ovary at the base.

The male stamens are tiny stalks, with pollen at the tip.

Petal

The ovary contains female eggs.

This drawing of the inside of a flower shows all of the parts that help it to reproduce.

A bee, with bright yellow pollen grains stuck to its legs, visits a flower on an apple tree (also called blossom).

Carrying pollen

Many plants rely on insects to spread their pollen. Flowers often use a sweet scented liquid called **nectar** to attract insects, such as bees. The insects visit flowers to drink the nectar. As the insect drinks, pollen grains stick to its body and legs. Some pollen will rub off on the stigma of the next flower the insect visits. The pollen joins with the eggs to fertilise them, so they can develop into seeds.

Bright purple lavender growing in a farmer's field.

 HAVE A GO
Use a magnifying glass to look at flowers in the park or garden. Flowers come in many shapes and colours. Can you see the parts labelled in the picture? Watch what happens if an insect visits the flower.

An almond nut growing on an almond tree. Nuts are not seeds, they are fruits.

Fruits

After the flower is fertilised its petals drop off. The hollow ovary at the base swells to form a fruit. The fertilised eggs inside develop into seeds. Fruits such as apples, pears and melons are soft and juicy. Fruits can also be hard, like an acorn, or wrapped in a hard case we call a nut.

? How do seeds develop? Turn the page to find out.

Apple blossom on an apple tree.

When apple blossom dies back, the ovary swells to form an apple.

Cut an apple in half to

Seeds

A seed contains everything a young plant needs to grow. Inside the outer case is the baby plant with its first root, stem and pair of leaves. The seed also contains a food store to keep the young plant going. Seeds only grow into young plants in the right conditions. They can survive for years before starting to sprout (p. 24).

Quick FACTS

• Flowering plants reproduce by making flowers, fruits and seeds.
• Pollen from one flower fertilises the eggs in a second flower, so it can make fruits.
• Seeds develop inside the fruits.

QUIZ TIME!

What do bees do with any pollen that has stuck to their legs when they return to their hive?

a. eat it
b. grow flowers with it
c. feed it to their young

Answer on page 32.

Make this

Make a pressed flower diary to record the flowers you spot at different times of the year.

Using recycled paper for the pages looks really funky and is kind to the environment, too.

1 To make the cover for your pressed flower diary, fold a stiff piece of A4 card in half.

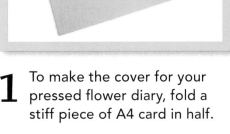

2 To make pages, fold lots of sheets of A4 paper in half. Then trim the pages so they are slightly smaller than the card. (You can have as many pages as you like.)

3 Place all the pages inside the card and fold in half again. Staple all the way down the fold so that the pages are secure.

4 Fill your diary with pressed flowers, poems, notes and drawings of flowers you have seen throughout the year.

SCATTERING AND SPROUTING

Plants need to scatter their seeds far and wide; they do this in different ways, using wind, water or animals.

Blowing on the wind

Plants spread their seeds so the young plants will grow in new places where there is space, light and moisture.

Thistledown and dandelion seeds are light enough to float on the wind. A breeze blows them away to new places. Ash and sycamore trees produce winged seeds that spin through the air like a helicopter when they fall from the tree.

Dandelion seeds have wispy parachutes that allow them to float on air.

HAVE A GO
Dandelion seeds are spread by the wind. Each small, light seed has a parachute of fine hairs. Find a dandelion that has gone to seed and blow on it. How many puffs does it take until all the seeds are gone?

Floating on water

Some plants that live by rivers or the seaside use water to scatter their seeds. Coconut palms grow on **tropical** beaches. Ripe coconuts fall into the water and float away. Tides and currents carry them to new beaches, where they may take root and grow.

A coconut on a beach has begun growing into a palm tree.

This waxwing will help to spread this plant's seeds by eating its juicy fruit.

Scattered by animals

Many plants rely on animals to spread their seeds. This can happen in two ways. Some plants produce seeds inside juicy fruits. When an animal eats the fruit, the seeds pass right through its body, and are left behind in its droppings. Plants such as burdock produce a prickly fruit called a **burr**. These burrs have tiny hooks that stick to animal fur. As the animals move around the burrs are carried to new places.

? What happens when seeds arrive in new places? Turn the page to find out.

A seed that has germinated grows its first new leaves and roots.

Sprouting and growing

Seeds that arrive in warm, light places with fertile soil will sprout and grow when the conditions are right. This is called **germination**. As the seed absorbs water it splits open. A tiny root grows downwards. Then a green shoot grows upwards, spreads its leaves and begins to make food. The young plant begins to grow.

QUIZ TIME!

If you eat an apple core, what happens to the seeds? Will they:

a. **pass through your body and disappear down the loo?**

b. **grow an apple tree in your tummy?**

c. **fly out of your nose when you sneeze?**

Answer on page 32.

Quick *FACTS*

• Plants use wind, water or animals to scatter their seeds.

• Seeds that reach warm, light places with good soil may begin to sprout, or germinate.

Himalayan balsam grows along riverbanks. Its seed pods explode and scatter seeds in all directions. The river then carries the seeds downstream until they find a place to sprout.

Make this

Cress is easy to grow from seed and it's tasty, too! Make a cool caterpillar cress container.

Put your caterpillar somewhere it will get some light – but not in direct sunlight. Make sure you keep the cotton wool damp. How long do you think it will take before your cress has grown and is ready to eat?

1 Cut the top off an egg box. Cut the bottom section in half.

2 Tape the sections together to form a long line.

3 Paint the outside green. Decorate with yellow spots. Bend a pipe cleaner in half, curl the ends and stick into the front section. Stick on two googly eyes.

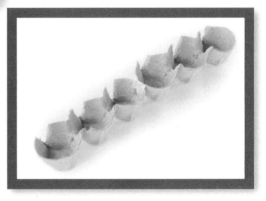

4 Put half a clean, dry eggshell into each section. Put damp cotton wool inside each eggshell. Sprinkle cress seeds onto the cotton wool.

USEFUL PLANTS

Plants are incredibly useful. They provide herbs, spices, medicines, most of our food and all kinds of other things!

Farmers in Vietnam, Asia, grow rice in fields covered with water, called paddy fields.

Crops

The plants we grow for food are called crops. These include **cereals**, such as rice, wheat, oats and barley. Trees and plants provide nuts and other fruits, such as apples, melons and bananas.

Other plants produce vegetables, such as peas and carrots. The drinks tea and coffee are made from plants. Chocolate is made from the beans of the cacao tree.

HAVE A GO

Take a look in your cupboards and fridge at home. How many of the foods you eat come from plants? You may be surprised by some of them. For example, pasta is often made from eggs, but it is also made using flour. The flour comes from a cereal called wheat.

Tree products

Trees are very useful plants. They provide timber, which is used to build houses and make furniture. Conifer trees produce softwood, while broad-leaved trees produce hardwood. Crushed wood chips are used to make paper and rubber is made from the milky **sap** of the rubber tree. Many things can be made from wood because it can be strong, light, bendy or hard and it is easy to form into different shapes.

Wood has been used to make most of the objects in this room – and the room itself!

Clothing and medicine

Plants, such as cotton, provide fibres that are spun to make clothing. Many medicines come from plants. Sap from poppies is used to make a painkiller called codeine. Aspirin was originally made from willow tree bark.

The white fluff that surrounds the seeds of the cotton plant is spun to make cotton.

? Which plants are used to flavour our food?
Turn the page to find out.

Herbs and spices

Herbs and spices are sometimes added to food to make it more tasty or colourful. Herbs, such as bay come from the green, leafy parts of plants. Spices, including mustard, are made from seeds, while cinnamon comes from bark. Chilli and peppercorns are fruits, turmeric comes from dried roots and saffron is actually the stigma of the crocus flower.

QUIZ TIME!

Beans are types of edible seed that grow in a:

a. **house**

b. **pod**

c. **pot**

Answer on page 32.

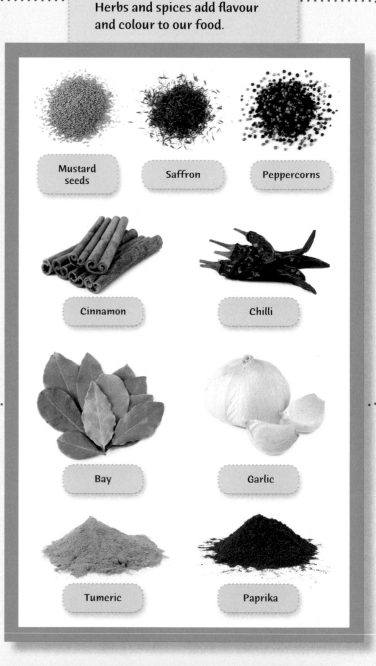

Herbs and spices add flavour and colour to our food.

Mustard seeds

Saffron

Peppercorns

Cinnamon

Chilli

Bay

Garlic

Tumeric

Paprika

Quick *FACTS*

• Plants provide much of our food.
• Herbs, spices, medicines and fibres for clothing all come from plants.
• Trees provide fruits, nuts, timber, paper and rubber.

Make this

Lolly sticks are made from thin, light wood. This wood is both light enough and strong enough to be turned into colourful fridge magnets.

You could add more designs to your fridge magnets, such as spots or wiggly lines.

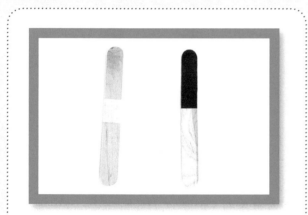

1 Wrap a piece of masking tape around the middle of some of your lolly sticks. Paint one end red. When they are dry remove the tape.

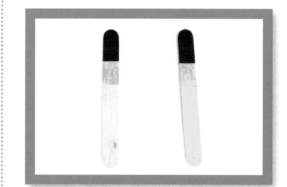

2 Line a piece of tape up with the red line on your lolly sticks and wrap it around the stick. Paint the wooden parts yellow. When they are dry remove the tape.

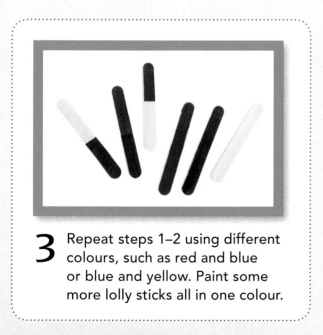

3 Repeat steps 1–2 using different colours, such as red and blue or blue and yellow. Paint some more lolly sticks all in one colour.

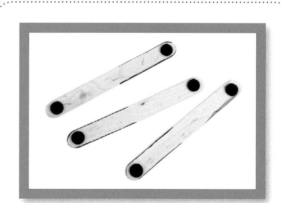

4 When dry, attach stick-on magnets to the unpainted sides, at both ends. Use the magnets to hold photos and notes on a fridge door.

GLOSSARY

absorb to take in

alpine something that lives in a mountain habitat

aquatic something that lives in or on water

Arctic the cold area around the North Pole

burr a seed with tiny hooks that catch onto animal fur, wool or onto people's clothing

carbon dioxide gas in the air, which plants use to make their food

cereals grain crops such as wheat, barley or rice

conifers a group of trees that produce cones containing seeds

crops plants that are grown especially for food or other uses

deciduous trees that lose their leaves every year

evergreens trees that keep their leaves all year

fertilised when male and female cells in a flower have joined and the plant can make seeds

fertiliser something that is full of nutrients, which is added to soil to help plants grow

germinate when a plant sprouts from a seed and starts to grow

habitat natural home of plants or animals, such as a forest or desert

irrigate when farmers water their fields in order to grow crops.

life cycle all the stages a living thing passes through before it dies

minerals natural, non-living substances

nectar sugary liquid that plants produce to attract insects

nutrients substances in food or minerals that help living things grow

ovary the hollow part of a flower, which forms the fruit containing the seeds

oxygen gas in the air that animals and people breathe, which plants produce as they make their food

photosynthesis process by which plants make their food using sunlight energy

pollen tiny grains produced by plants in order to make seeds

reproduction the process through which living things produce young

sap the sticky liquid inside the trunk and branches of a tree or other plant

shrub woody plant that is smaller than a tree

solar energy energy from the Sun

stamen male part of a flower that produces pollen. Stamens look like little stalks

stigma female part of a flower that receives pollen

tropical places in the hot regions of the world, found near the Equator

veins tiny tubes in a leaf that carry food and water

BOOKS

Lifecycles: From Seed to Sunflower
by Dr Gerald Legg (Franklin Watts, 2014)

See How Plants Grow: series
by Nicola Edwards (Wayland, 2012)

Earth Cycles: Plants
by Sally Morgan (Franklin Watts, 2012)

Nature Trail: series
by Jen Green (Wayland Books, 2010)

Outdoor Explorers: Planting and Growing
by Sandy Green (Franklin Watts, 2013)

WEBSITES

http://library.thinkquest.org/3608/
A fun website that explains how plants live and grow.

http://resources.woodlands-junior.kent. sch.uk/revision/science/living/plants.html
This school website has funky games and activities about plants.

http://www.artistshelpingchildren.org/ flowersgardenartscraftsideassprojectskids
This website is full of craft projects and activities relating to plants.

http://www.greatgrubclub.com
Hints and tips on this website will help you grow flowers, fruits and vegetables.

NOTE TO PARENTS AND TEACHERS:

Every effort has been made by the Publishers to ensure that these websites are suitable for children, that they are of the highest educational value, and that they contain no inappropriate or offensive material. However, because of the nature of the Internet, it is impossible to guarantee that the contents of these sites will not be altered. We strongly advise that Internet access is supervised by a responsible adult.

INDEX

QUIZ ANSWERS

Page 5: **c** – carrot. (Mushrooms are not plants, they are fungi.)

Page 8: **b** – wilting.

Page 12: **c** – petals are actually brightly coloured leaves.

Page 16: **a** – Hyperion. (The General Sherman is the world's biggest tree, but it is not the tallest.)

Page 20: **c** – they feed it to their young.

Page 24: **a** – they pass through your body and disappear down the loo.

Page 28: **b** - pod.